The Bouquet Race: My Overture

NOBLE LEE LESTER

DEDICATION

This is dedicated to God for allowing me to invest, deposit and participate in your presence & hopefully your future if not through me others. There is hope for our world healing; healing to become what God has launched us to fulfill. Why must we heal; because all 7 of my children, and their children, are amazing? They will need liberation elbow-room to blossom.

CONTENTS

ACKNOWLEDGMENTS

A Prelude (from my father):

This book (The Bouquet Race series: My Overture) is a series of chapter pieces about Black people—African-Americans-inspired by my dad, Steve Lester, who didn't particularly favor the various race titles, names, epithets and descriptions given to us/him during his time (1920 thru 2010). He had an amazing culture shock shared by my mother, Seanna, during their honeymoon trip in Atlanta, Ga. in the 1940's They not only met "beautiful lookin' Negro peoples" everywhere but unlike most of the rural areas of Valdosta, Georgia, and Thomasville Alabama where they were from, at that time, were also highly educated, professional and socially refined in African cultures. He never forgot those unprecedented civil anomalies; African oddities to him if you will, "these beautiful, good looking peoples" in that way he would address them. What did he see so different, so pure and refined? Perhaps their dignity shining through, their relishing of freedom to be, do and go where they pleased? He was so astonished he thought he'd privately rename them different from the national labels they'd been inappropriately labeled to "The Bouquet Race." He'd deed something he thought more deserving that he hadn't seen in the local "Negroes or Color people" he grew up among. My father would often say, "Negro peoples is a like a bouquet of flowers, Nobah. We are all different; all kind of colors and shades." Like my father, I am not a spokesman for shades and hues of Black people but I am an appreciator of the misrepresented cultures they hail from and all the influences left me.

What is this book about? **How to love Black People.**

I thank you in advance for reading these series and sharing my father's sentiments and empirically raw wisdom

CHAPTER 1
POEM

BLACK PEOPLE NEED A HUG:
God, you are absolutely right!

"I am responsible for my actions"

But boy could I use a hug

After 450 years of rambling, confused by what happened, what went wrong and where did I land Lord?

I could still use a hug

Sure, someone thought it wrong to enslave men in a free land; a land that I hear fights for that very cause elsewhere yet the men who lost that united contradictory fight has blamed me... because why again...?

I sure could use that hug right now

I know I'm a shattered mirror and I am trying to collect my broken pieces and fuse them back together again that I might see an image of my true self again but I can't remember ever seeing myself before I got lost

Dag! ...Excuse me, but I could use a drink too with that hug

You are right, "I really need to learn to pull myself up and get over it and try and move on—because life does move on after all"

But man oh man God, could I use just one little hug

You're right after the hose blast me, the dog bit me and my boss man violated my daughters, I shouldn't have hit him back. It's my fault I'm in jail with other J-walkers just like me

You are right. But dear God I'm fadin', when can I get that hug

a. Grandfather and Grandmother Orson & Leila Mae Barfield wedding picture.

THE BOUQUET RACE: MY OVERTURE

Chapter 2

Back in the day

Sometimes I go back to my hometown, Trenton, NJ.

And I stroll through the historical Washington parks, walk on the old brick and cobblestone paved streets and recall my younger years of coming home from a house party at night or window shopping outside the downtown stores that I loved; lusting over Italian knitted sweaters and shark-skin trousers. I'd always reflect back-in-the-day when I marched the streets with the famous Cavalier Drill Team in the 1960's:

1 Young little me above, 1964, second from the left.

2 Photo at the War Memorial building

3 Local parade East State St

4 Madman El Cid

5 The local parades

6 Colonel Bingham, center, its founder & originator

Wow! Back when the amazing marching Cavaliers were the toast of the town, where I began my show-business career, I guess you could say.

　　　The Cavaliers were so popular the city's parade masters were forced to put us at the end of every parade event. Like a good pipe piper, all of the parade viewers would follow us to the very end, Black and White Trentonians alike. We actually outshined, "(Humphrey) Hogart'd," commandeered and upstaged every other parade participant: the famous

Fort Dix Army base rifle twirlers,　　　　　　　　the McGuire

8

Air-force Base marching band airmen, the

Mummer's and Elk parade exhibits, the

Eastern stars and Masons. We all were part of the many proud things that hailed out of Trenton, NJ—but The Cavaliers were the national award winning drilling highlight, one of the wonders of the world.

I also like to visit the old neighborhood taverns like the Passaic Street Candlelight Lodge, the Calhoun Street Tuxedo Club and observe the changes that time and life has brought upon people I knew and grew up with. I like to watch the folks and all the changes go by. I still find it amazing how people changed so much; some for the better and others, well, unfortunately not so much sadly.

Trenton was a town with prized people from all walks of life; real class acts all around. They had style, swag and flamboyant personalities in abundance, Black and White. I enjoyed observing their colorful characteristics: the Broad and State Street players, the Italian "Fonzie" leather jacket motorcades, revving their V8 engines and sporting their wet Vitalis hair-dos, the big-legged bobby-sock Catholic schools girls giggling on the corner of State and Broad.

The Chamberburg Italian kids were the coolest. They were amazing soccer players. The "Fonze" had nothing on their sporty leather goods and south-Philly garments.

The merchant bakeries, Cheese-steaks & Hoagie shops and a sundry of stores had the nicest people in the world, and oh, and the best tomato pies.

We adored the Princeton-Day school, Lawrenceville and Hun School preppy kids and their really cool Oxford penny-loafers, the Ivy League beige khaki-trousers, navy blue blazers, P-coats, wool socks and

wool Scottish tames.

The Jewish community and shops were my parents' best friends. The massive pastrami kraut sandwiches, elephant ear pastry and fresh cut breads and bagels, the best. And, they ALWAYS gave you too much of everything to eat. I loved these communities and especially all their differences.

People watching and checking people out was something I inherited from my foster folks, my guardian parents—the Lester's. So, I'm clear, and I'll talk more about this, but I was adopted at the age of two. My biological mother, her husband, and I have reunited at 19 years but more about that later. They called it, "watchin'," or some called it, "digging the scene," "reading a crowd."

My foster folks were avid people watchers. They'd sit for hours parked in various neighborhoods, but mostly parked at the Battle Monument, i.e., 5 Points, stretch where the famous 5 roads came together: Warren, Pennington, Brunswick and Princeton Avenues. It was a monument that saluted the triumph of George Washington and his defeat over the British invaders at the Delaware Riverfront.

5 Points was a crossroads if there ever was one. My parents would, what appeared mundane to me, observe passer-by's comings and goings. It was a regular weekend routine for them.

7 George Washington's monument at 5 points

8 The NJ state's capital

Although I never really understood what my parents' "watchin'" intentions were during those times, but boy were they nosey to a fault, I thought. Perhaps they observed people simply for entertainment, boredom relief or maybe they had their "business" reasons unbeknown to me as a child, like: who had the "goods," i.e., "hot items" (windfalls, stolen goods) street sales (side-a-beef, pork chops or chicken parts and fresh fish in bulk) or clothes, poker game connections or their biggest hustle, number running.

I was nothing more than a wee husky sized lad back then in the late 1950's whose dreams were only of my next order of French Fries, unofficial bicycle and skate street race tournaments, daydreaming along the Raritan Canal bank watching minnows, trekking bare-feet curiously along the river, fishing for Sunnies and skipping flat rocks across the Delaware River.

9a Parent's 2nd floor Jewish flat, Market & Cooper Sts, 8 years old.

My parents' street business could have been anything. It was all about survival for better living for my sister Cora and myself. Having been the grand-children of former slaves, my folks had learned wisely what they had to do to survive the contempt of racism that loath after them socially. They took nothing for granted.

They had a knack for hustle. My folks were not above "workin' the streets"--we're not talking The Black Bourgeoisie or the Talented Tenth academician Negro scholars from the classy Westside or Ewing Townships of Trenton--far from it. They were everyday regular down-home folks; the hub of good-heartedness and visceral lifestyles. They lived by it, respected it and survived the streets because of it--quite brilliantly I might add, passing it on to me.

Watching them "watch," or observe, people was sometimes an exciting ordeal. It was the cheapest admission free entertainment that money could buy.

Weekend Fridays were traditionally when "the eagle flies high," i.e., "PAY-DAY," for the local blue collar "Negro" Trentonian laborers. All who were paid was out in full force happy and filled to bursting with excitement--at least feelin' free for the next two days (Friday & Saturday nights) to do their "thang" and get their "groove on."

"Party hardy ya'll!!" Was the nightly mantra. It wasn't quite the Mardi Gras but it was her 1st cousin bosom buddy.

This would echo the streets and bars all night; shaking off the stress of the da' *man* after a long week of tolerating his crazy-ass was needed therapy. They needed "cracker-relief" from the white boss-man. It was that or kill Mr. Gilmo', one or the other. But interesting enough, with all the hardship and stress on Colored People, they managed never to talk about harming, revolting or attacking White people--NEVER. The media always reported how Blacks rioted and ram-shacked their "own" neighborhood but never reported how frustrated Coloreds became as result of mistreatment and "legal" police abuse. Kicking Black-folk ass was a political ploy for whites to get reelected. Black people just ignored them, and believe it or not Ripley, Blacks felt sorry for Whites actually.

Blacks would pity them: they lacked body movement, humanity, spirit and soul. They needed to get drunk or excommunicated in order to let loose in the way Blacks behaved naturally. Like an animal that smell things miles ago, hear the faintest sounds or spot an annoying gnat yards away. Black people would shake their heads at this lack of perception and go on with their work. Like a wild animal Blacks were able to snap them in half but didn't because they knew not what they do—or they were staring down the barrel of more than just one Muhammad Ali, Mike Tyson or

Sonny Liston in this era's case.

They'd hold out partying for as long as their limited weekend cash would afford them or until the "licka'" (alcohol) stop flowing.

Generally, the weekly ritual for most men was to stop off home once they "knocked off" (dismissed from work at 5:00 pm) and give "momma," i.e., their woman, wife or their significant-other, common-law partner or "shacker," some cash.

You see back then, Tthe bed was seriously undefiled." Neighbors, you didn't know, or cared about you, would approach you and advocate your immoral sin or wrong-doings. Oh sure, they had shacking-up going on back then but only on the "down-low." That was a big taboo, a no-no among decent God-fearing folks. An honest man was expected to make his "girl" an "honest woman," if he was to live with her or "sleep-over" from time to time.

From his handed-over pay check, momma would allowance him his play-cash for his debts, i.e., numbers played "on time," (credit for that week) and a little gambling cash perhaps. And more than likely, he'd probably had a little stashed away (tips & side hustles), plus a "few dollahs" to get his "drank-on" (alcohol). Nevertheless, the respectful protocol was to bring money home ta' momma from the week's pay to secure clean clothes, a meal of butter beans and ham-hocks during the week. This was the definition of a real man back then who'd work hard all week, and come Friday or Saturday, it was playing time! Sunday, however, was due to the Lord.

Life was not bad in Trenton then. However, economically racism never allowed Blacks to get ahead by systemic and political design. Neither the North nor the Southerners could tolerate Blacks getting financially or politically advanced in general, but Blacks ALWAYS managed to get by, and thanks to mayoral advances like Douglas Palmer, Tony F. Mack, and Eric Jackson Trenton has managed to change that paradigm.

Pimps in Trenton were another stronghold issue for the church. Believe it or not, young men, and myself, aspired to be prominent pimps— "Superfly" in TNJ. This was a very real aggrandizing but degenerating dream for most players. Now historically, pimps supplied whites-Johns with red-light frolics, "Honky" action and fresh entertainment. There was an unspoken myth among white men; "a white boy wasn't a man until he laid a Black woman." "Honkies" were usually rich white men who'd park in front of a "red-light establishment" and *honk* for service—hence, **Honky**. There an accommodating respectable, but extravagantly dressed gentleman would escort some well garnished "action-piece" to the inquiring car until the caller found visual satisfaction. What was so lucrative about this gig, the pimp was frequently "untouchable" by law: Judges, politicians', police, clergymen, firemen, etc., would all collude to this end. The job benefits consist of selective professions offering a well-managed concierge of professional protection, this was a gainful career indeed. A pimp in Trenton was compared to a Hollywood actor. Black men would pray for such an ill-repute position and calling. This bubbled Teflon protection alone was an incentive to grope after. It was a dangerous job of course but good study-work nevertheless with assorted pleasures from the powerful. Turning a blind eye to flesh-crimes was a necessary investment to guard the reputation of the upper-upper middle class. If a pimp screwed up horribly, *people* in high-places would turn a deaf ear to his indiscretions. He might find himself in a vat of flesh solvent. There were a lot of pup-pimps whom disappeared with nothing more than fading memory of their existence--gone.

Mum's the word for the prohibition-speakeasy as well; after hours drinking clubs and such. Pimps and pushers all got a golden brick road to travel upon. "What happens on the ship stays there"—this went without saying. If a loose lip sunk a ship, you got a bullet in the Cerebral-Cortex and vat douse courtesy of the Newark shore docks.

Pimps needed their hierarchy, social rank and prissy class—they had their very own "pimp-laugh." Therefore, the pussy-peddler, cunt-curator must have his opulence. This was allowed and yet an illegal deaf ear waived it away and left it unturned. While they flaunted their earnings with fur coats, glittered-girls, and customized built cars, no one interfered provided he supplied the demand and kept his mouth shut.

As for the commoners, the law was hard, fast and clear 'no one could enslave Negroes legally but the law never said one had to pay them reasonably or fairly.' I can't prove it but it was clear the wealthy all collude to pay the Negro nothing--the glass-ceiling was painted over. Negroes and Coloreds earned just enough to make it week-to-week but not enough to quit and certainly not enough to go on sabbatical. Frankly that was unheard of. One ran the risk of pissing off jealous white co-workers daring to have cash enough for leisure. Whites made some exception with clergy types however but not too much or too frequently. Their motive there was to keep the powerful-animals jaded and docile waitin' on da' Lord to come back to fight their battle. White racism ran deeply and unfortunately continues to run on. Whites seemingly NEVER wanted anyone below their station appearing to be better than they—a sad side effect of capitalism. It was real American apartheid. A mastermind plan whites were never wise enough to figure out how was equally destroying them too.

My father not taking vacations with his wife put a serious wedge in their marriage at times my mother never understood. Again, not taking a vacation was an act of employment survival for him. Just one uppity ill-fated conduct like a vacation would ruin him with contempt and jeopardize his families' livelihood. "What shiftless choice is this to get away from whites on holiday?" A wife not understanding her husband's environmental pressures—which a lot of men Black men repressed--could cause him his job. For these reasons, Black men drank incessantly--Blacks made Dewar's scotch quite wealthy during the '50's thru the '90's. Many were not willing to admit to their families the stress they suffered trying to be a man. How does a man socialize unspoken rules of obstruction to his family? A vacation for my father was an illusion. What boss would pay a Black man to relax for a week? Could the boss afford to even let that get out among white subordinates? My father just made the most of Sundays and national holidays after 20 years. During the 1950's thru the late 1960's he had to work 7 days a week. It wasn't until the mid-'60's he got Saturday and Sunday off with pay. I now know why my father fell asleep at every opportunity. I hated him for being so sleepy and not willing catch with me.

In the case of my mother, he would endorse her Floridian frequent flights (I mean drives) and sent her on her way but she was left alone too much quite often dragging me along or my brother Spencer. Loneliness can have a duel edge blade on a spouse. I'm sure they both felt lonely. I am not certain but an extramarital affair may have snaked in their lives for this very racial side effect they had no control over and was forced to tolerate as Black minorities coping with northern apartheid.

The socio-political system in Trenton was laid out perfectly bias. Jews, although red-lined away from protestant White-Americans were able to set up businesses within the Colored-Negro community confounds as well as Italians, Polish and low-profiling Germans too.

And, speaking of Germans, I was a grown man before I realized why Germans in our neighborhood very seldom exited their homes; peeking from behind their curtains; often steering away from the convenient Jewish shops in our community. We children thought their aloofness was because they were really haunted, witches, or they didn't like the sun. I also thought maybe they were afraid of us: "Colored People." Subsequently, this was the late 1950's and Nazi war criminals were still at large being sought after readily by Israeli secret Interpol, so I would gather later. Perhaps they were afraid of being profiled as innocent war criminals knowing what their country had done to annihilate a race of people. Or, maybe we harbored Nazi criminals under the Jewish business community nose? It was pretty clear Whites did not favor Jews during this era. More than likely ex-WWII negro soldiers knew better but a lot were bitter after fighting such a war in Europe to come back to racial mistreatment perhaps a lot of them turned a blind eye. Let the incognito Krauts be—enough blood shed.

Trentonian White-businesses were racially endorsed and lumped all together. Their business endeavors were encouraged for the good of local and national economy. But, it was always implied "the coloreds" would not prosper in business or be endorsed by local banks and investment machinery. This was clear. Spilling blood isn't the only form of annihilation. However, other than barbers, undertaking, beauty shops and perhaps a bar or two, Blacks were green-light to provide service, provided they were self-financed.

Jewish Synagogue (Nathan Barnert Memorial)

Nonetheless, the blacks accepted defecting foreigners wholeheartedly, we surrounded them, and got along with them—we adored their differences. It was whites who pretend to be indifferent to our soul-food, dance floors, gospel, Jazz and Blues, our dress, our swag and expressed passion for worship. Their Rock n Roll they loved provided a white covered the song.

Ironically, we enjoyed their fresh rye bread, bagels, Rueben sandwiches, pickled tomatoes and cucumbers, "tomato pies" (pre-pizza), Koshered poultry, fresh produce, gouda and cheddar cheeses and that awful smell of gefilte fish curing. We bought their goods, protected them and made them rich deliberately--willingly. Blacks were well aware of what they were economically doing for them which Seanna, my foster mother, took full and total advantage of. My mother is the ONLY person I knew who could "out-jew" (haggle) a Jew. Again, I speculate to think that's probably why Blacks burn down foreigner's stores during the social-riots of civil unrest and the killings of MLK, Malcolm X, Medgar Evers and John & Robert Kennedy, men in prison and the "strange-fruit." The many foreigners had proven they would not stand with Blacks or by them during civil rights protest, public challenges, and general mistreatment. They conveniently separated and racially trend against us in hopes they'd get invited into the white cash flow—and it worked. So, I think that's why we trashed them. And, they grabbed their insurance money and fled.

Negroes were always limited by glass ceiling issues both north and south. They felt they could not advance beyond their more accepted White immigrant class. Although the immigrants were from different countries, Blacks later in the late 1960's and early 1970's ran the risk of annoying the foreigners with uppity social stations. Our discriminated Jews and blocked out Italians did not mind living near us, or serving us. They accepted our money. In fact, they had very little choice because we were in part their main source of income. But however, to see us better off than they also troubled their southern-minded connections with indigenous Whites who'd migrated into New Jersey. They too were trying to survive white-racism and their self-destructive false superiority nonsense.

Their cognitive dissonant issues (*In psychology, cognitive dissonance is the mental stress or discomfort experienced by an individual who holds two or more contradictory beliefs, ideas, or values at the same time, performs an action that is contradictory to one or more beliefs, ideas or values, or is confronted by new information that conflicts with existing beliefs, ideas, or values.* {Intrigued and enamored by blacks but left with no choice but to hate them.}) wouldn't allow them social respect for HBCU's like Howard University and Spelman, or Lincoln, Morehouse, Fisk, Florida A&M, Xavier, Hampton, etc., when it was their separatism that necessitated these institutions. To them, these schools were inferior unaccredited institutions. Now, ironically, poor foreigners and immigrants frequent these fine professional institutes like dentistry, law, sociology and medical schools because of obvious cost effectiveness coupled with a fine education and certifiable training. Moreover, most immigrants didn't like racism and bigotry. Many, upon arrival, after intimately socializing with Negro GI's, were shocked to know this social terrorism and political-dirt existed under the fine rugs of white Americans. Many never held of such bigotry. Hell, it was the very thing many defected from; their own sterilization, gag orders and Stalin-starvation tactics. Once here, most were lead and coerced to undermine Black's worth as a prerequisite to being an American citizen—for their own survival, they behaved accordingly with biases and discrimination.

Nevertheless, back to Black male and female relations, as meager as a Black man's paycheck may have been, life was better when "momma," the wife or live-in girlfriend had her economic weekly bills-paid securely, balances cleared, i.e., her on-time (credit) groceries, her rent, and her church tithes, alms and offerings were set. She was then a happier camper.

During the '60's these weekend characters were "off-the-chain": colorful, idle-wild, creative, self-expressing and living a roaring lifestyle you would not believe. Everybody had a sporty but cool walk and a slick poetic talk all their own. Hey, after such a long, arduous and stressful week of handling the "Man" and all his barking demands, Friday night frolics was the steam-valve that released pressures that kept some of them mildly sane.

9 Brawls would breakout when Blacks crossed the neighborhood color line.

This boulevard (5 points) was a floor show for most Trentonians including my mom and dad. It was sometimes better than the county-fair side-shows. There they were some of the most interesting and funniest characters I have yet to meet in show-business. 5 points was "Comedy Central," the "comic revue" and "comedy unleashed" live with no commercials. They were hilarious, competing and vying for laughs. They were funnier than any TV show: The Honey-Mooners, Sanford & Son, Archie Bunker and the Jefferson's rolled into one; a hoot and a holla' all-night long; on the floor belly laughter. It was a healthy means to emotionally survive systemic hardship and random uninvited trouble. Look, this was way of coping with the many disappointments of a contradictory ill-America.

Grown men would "street-box" (non-lethal play fighting) to the body as it were. This was crafty, harmless sparring horse-play among guys that limited itself to fist targets below the neck. It would always draw a crowd. Much like sparring martial artist, they kept score with the oozes and ahhs of onlookers dressed in their finest Italian knits and sharkskin Saturday night-outfits while exercising their lightning-fast hands. This was more valve-relieving of angst steam.

Do-Wop singers showcased on virtually every corner harmonizing nothing but romantic love songs of woo. They were sung with impeccable harmonics, with stylish routines and moves, and perfect to thrilling choreography.

The famous Jitterbug, he was a cool-cat aggrandizer who'd rapped (poet talk) in a style of rhymes and rhythm always talking in a linguistic code of prose based on street wit, puns and fun with "hipness" he'd ascertained from Newark, NYC or Chicago. These cats were smooth operators: fast on their feet, dance-happy and slipping and sliding on the club's dance floor sipping gin and juice. They would take the dance over with the "Mash-Potatoes," the "Cha, cha, cha," or the "Slop" while others just promenaded through "uptown" 5 points, at the Battle Monument stylizing so they might look better than they felt deep inside.

5 points, (Warren St, Broad St, Pennington Ave., Princeton Ave. {now Martin Luther King, Jr. Boulevard} and Brunswick Avenues) the crown of Trenton doing their thing on the streets of New Jersey's inner capital city.

Chapter 3

Red-lines and class lines

In the United States, **redlining** is the practice of denying services, either directly or through selectively raising prices, to residents of certain areas based on the racial or ethnic makeups of those areas. While some of the most famous examples of redlining regard denying financial services such as banking or insurance,[2] other services such as healthcare [3] or even supermarkets,[4] can be denied to residents to carry out redlining.[5] The term "redlining" was coined in the late 1960s by John McKnight, a sociologist, and community activist.[6] It refers to the practice of marking a red line on a map to delineate the area where banks would not invest; later the term was applied to discrimination against a particular group of people (usually by race or sex) irrespective of geography.

During the heyday of redlining, the areas most frequently discriminated against were black inner city neighborhoods. For example, in Atlanta in the 1980s, a Pulitzer Prize-winning series of articles by investigative-reporter Bill Dedman showed that banks would often lend to lower-income whites but not to middle- or upper-income blacks.[7] The use of blacklists is a related mechanism also used by red-liners to keep track of groups, areas, and people that the discriminating party feels should be denied business or aid or other transactions. In the academic literature, redlining falls under the broader category of credit rationing.

Reverse redlining occurs when a lender or insurer targets nonwhite consumers, not to deny them loans or insurance, but rather to charge them more than could be charged to a comparable white consumer.[8] [1]

During my growing up era, the 19 50 thru 1970's, the red-lined sections and areas denoted typical locations for most Blacks to live, if not all African-Americans. The Red-Line effect covered every area of Trenton the North, South, East and West Trenton. However, the city, to its credit, was fairly diverse during these periods and time-lines. Different class of Blacks choose to live and discriminate among each other ironically, not necessarily having the political and financial power to red-line a sampled

---

[1] Wikipedia, the free dictionary, 2016

group, but choosing to live away from so-called social "riff-raff" and common-types so-called "n-word" categories if you will.

North Trenton had many great locations but essentially 5 points were its hot-hub. It had rows of narrow multi-level antiquated attached residential houses and some project buildings (Frazier Homes & Calhoun Street projects, etc.). There were several red-light zoning (quasi-legal prostitution) and lots of angry and impoverished communities of record violence and crime. To my limited knowledge, North and East Trenton were the initial narcotic targets and drug infested outbreak of illegal drugs. Although, the North-side had many educated, middle-class minded Negroes mixed with Native-Indian blood that migrated and lived in project housing. I dated a girl, Judy Walker, who was derivative of this Lawrenceville lot and we shared a child: Tara P Gray.

South Trenton had its share of project-public housing environments also. Blacks there coexisted with surrounding strong working class European numbers—impoverished and poorly educated whites, struggling to live also. They took advantage of the south side steel mill jobs and industry employment along the Delaware river; as well as shops and stores that had no choice but to cater to Black clientele. Generally these same working-class whites, who didn't typically take part in other ethnic businesses or socially mix with them publicly, other than the skating rink on Lalor St., never gave me any feeling they were grateful for Black support but they were fools to discriminate against their economic base. We bought their Spam, hog-head cheese, bologna, bubble gum and cigars. Clearly, the "ghetto-whites" were being discriminated against by the West-Trenton white mainstream. So, what was the point of perpetuated prejudice against Blacks and their wallets? We bought everything from them even their imported drugs.

So we're clear, when I refer to class, I mean specifically financial quotient, the therewithal to cash, income and economic flow. I don't wish to cast any belittling dispersions of stations, hue or lack of social acceptance.

East Trenton had a smattering of lower-middle-class Black families but mostly strong religious church going contingencies—a number of Holinesses (Holy-rollers) churches. They too lived near the many factories on the Clinton Avenue stretch of that time, factories now defunct and mostly abandon, but this was their means of income and livelihood—working for Jewish factories.

West Trenton had your college educated; lighter skin, ex-military Euro-wedded progressive school teachers, prison guards, State Psychiatric Hospitable, or those who worked for the city and civil service type Negroes. However, West Trenton's racial line of demarcation and red-line divide began separating them at Cadwalader Park & Parkside Avenue due west of Jr #3 middle school. There the elite Trentonians lived and among the surrounding townships of Hilltonia, Hill Crest, Lawrenceville, and Parkside. Ewing Township for example, (a West Trenton borough) they were inhabited by the Black Bourgeoisie and their middle-class split-level, duplexes, sunken living-rooms, two car garages and mostly ranch house dwellings, etc.

We Blacks lived with so much geo-segregation in Trenton, here in the so-called "free north." The south was never a real culture shock to most Blacks who ventured below the Mason-Dixon Line --it wasn't much of an adjustment from there to Trenton. Things were peaceful for many years while Blacks and Whites stayed in their places. Ironically, we were equally worse for the wear in our so-called "places": blacks violently cutting each other, Italians and their drive-bys, Jews cheating one another and Germans and Poles pretending to blend in with Catholics.

White mainstream only became a problematic issue when Blacks wanted political power, class bank loans for industry and higher education from private institutions like Ivy League school access. It was the endorsement of liberal-minded hippies from politically endowed families advocating equality for Blacks that ruffled their feathers with pushback. Well, they lost that fight. And now, it's not so much an issue but more of an on-the-fence benevolence.

Again, we were lumped together because of their "mom and pop" (Mah & Paw) storefronts that provided and exploited the Coloreds and Negroes. But, it was cool—really--and it still is, even with the discriminated Arabs (Muslims, Coptic & Christian-Arabs) who has taken the place of Jews in our neighborhoods, for the very same political ramifications, selling their goods and wares. Black people really had/have no issue with cultural and color differences. The black and white thing was a white-American problem. I haven't nailed their problem convincingly—is it genetic survival? Are they afraid of NOT being white any longer?

Sure, ALL LIVES MATTER but Black laws, medicine, organ extraction or prisons aren't taking White lives. Black cops aren't killing white children. Blacks have and are still supporting everybody yet—they still spending money, votes, renting your movies, and kicking up your TV ratings; and for what? It was they, the invisible Anglo-whites who allowed, endorsed and zoned the aforementioned "immigrants" (Jews, Poles, and Italians) to eke out a livelihood in Black hoods. But, again, it was okay with Blacks. They are still there for you.

Clearly, I can see where the great African kings and kingdoms of Mali, Songhai and Ghanaian empire states, before the Egyptian empire fell, were known for too much humanity, embrace and trust of the foreigner Arabs and Portuguese human traders. When kingdoms fell, they swooped in and took full advantage.

Look, Black people simply want *inclusion*. Slavery was/is a nagging emotional dandruff-flake on our Sunday-go-to-meeting clothes we were/are still brushing away. Blacks weren't interested in conquering, sacking and pillaging White people—a coup was never an agenda—not even the FOI, the Black Panthers, any liberation group or riots. That was pure anger and frustration for blatant injustice. All Blacks didn't cheer OJ's triumphant but they did cheered beating the pants off the law that has forever abused Blacks. No matter how angry Black people became at their white brothers there were no plans for expressed physical animosity toward whites. Blacks were always humane. The only time white people got a clear ass-whoopin' was in the boxing ring. The ring was the line of demarcation. "Danger, Wil Robinson, beat-down just ahead." Again, they only wanted to feel **included** that their BLACK LIVES did MATTER.

Blacks fought world wars, won Olympic Games and won ballgames. # **42**, Jackie Robinson, suffered "n-word" heckling from a northern Phillies' manager, from Philadelphia, in "The city of brotherly love" of all places. Brown people just wanted a hug of approval—to be in—a break from the running, hiding, proving, begging, sucking up, unprivileged feelings and praying to God for validation.

Blacks straightened, conked and iron pressed their hair to blend in and assimilate with white likeness. They tried as near and dear as possible to escape their looks most whites thought frightening—so they thought. These cosmetic adjustments were to show America our physical worth.

I recall an embarrassing but passionate conversation from one of my parent's roomers (a lodger) gloating over his attractive looks bragging that, "If only he had blue eyes also, like a white man, and long straight hair. Who?! Lord have mercy! He would be a killer pimp." It was this married U.S. Army man's wish to be Caucasian to dazzle exploited women to better serve mankind in his flesh trade fantasies bragging in his wife's presence. These were frequent talks I'd hear from neighbors amass growing up in Trenton, NJ.

The evidence was desperately clear. Black people wanted nothing more than to be accepted—included. "I want to be white in my next life." "If only I were white, I would...!" These were just a few outbursts of daily degenerating exhilarations I heard as a child and young man. They were willing to be the red-headed stepchild, even in the north, just to feel accepted. And, no matter how hard my father and his peers tried to move up, to be counted, and doing the right thing, was for not. There was never enough soup for poor Oliver Twist as he continued to straighten and Gerri-Curl his wonderfully powerful beautiful woolly hair.

Trevor Noah, a south African mulatto of German blood, anchors for the comedy series "The Daily Show," wrote a hilarious book where he honors his south-African mother trying to raise a half white child during the apartheid racist-regime madness. "The family sat, about to eat, and the mother elected the grandmother to pray—to say grace. The grandmother rejected the opportunity and reelected Trevor. She seriously begun to rationale that since Trevor was ½ white, and God doesn't listen to Blacks, maybe Trevor could get a prayer through since whites have it all." Trevor's story was hilariously expressed but the truth of the matter it was a sad.

In my day, there was only one funeral home in Trenton, NY, Dr. Anderson's at Calhoun St & Pennington Ave and two Black own restaurants, Tom Woddenberry's, the only one I recall in the 1960's located right at 5 points. Any effort to seek funding to enterprise often was not prospering. Banks knew white people (middle class and up with the money) were not going to cater to Negro business. Black on Black money didn't count to the banks—Their excuse: "It was a poor investment." And sadly, many Negroes were reluctant to comply and support local Black businesses also other than barber shops and hair parlors. However, what the whites did do for "Black business," is hire housekeepers who were essentially in-house chefs, baby-sitters or laundry maids. This employment included my mother, my aunts, and my sister. Blacks carried much faith in White immigrant enterprises and less their own. Actually, it was Blacks across the nation in big cities, back then, that started the wealth among many Jews, Italian, German and Polish immigrants as powerful as they are today. Blacks catered to their little storefronts of cold cuts, soda and cigarettes, shoe shops, millineries, pawn shops, Kosher deli's, mini-grocery stores, drugstore fountain, package goods, tomato pie shops, roller-rinks, cab companies, credit-driven furniture stores and Jewish bakeries.

Blacks would sometimes outright brag about their immigrate support. "Hey, I git your hands off my knit (Italian sweater) I got this downtown at "Buyers Men Shop" on Broad and Hanover Streets" or South

Street in Philly. These were popular cool-clothing stores for men that Blacks held in high esteem.

Everybody had their place, had "the hook-up" and most knew the deal. Blacks were to be a host for the struggling immigrant parasites as they forged their empires via "our" neighborhoods and Blacks were the discount benefactors. Whites were NOT coming to any inner city stores.

In business, Blacks had odd stigmas charged against them. They were often criticized with lacking bedside-manners toward their own. They were often accused of lacking hospitality, being unable to smile, expecting the bad behavior (a fight or argument) and mistreating "their kind": "They so uppity" "Their prices are too high there." "I guess he thinks he's the head (n-word) in charge." "They don't know how to talk to anybody when you do support them!" "I think they're putting water in the liquor, myself" — and self-boycotting. As well, some Blacks would resent one another, reacting with jealousy toward business-minded progressives for moving too far ahead to fast. It was frightening to know that advancing or being educated was a real threat. This was debilitating. Who could prosper with constant shots-in-the-foot? In many ways, we were duplicating the behavior of the racist Klan mentality.

Often, the frustration of supplies failing to meet meager demands, poor bank backing and Blacks forced to buy retail because wholesaler's and credit unions not extending favors readily to people of color. Yet, the first opportunity any "white-immigrant" got to assimilate into the mainstream, step up his empire, or move up and out of the hood, they were gone in a flash without a good-bye. Sometimes they would actually behave as if they'd done Blacks a favor by being there. Truth be told, Blacks loved, needed and protected them.

In the 1960's, Trenton had a two-hour local radio show of "Colored music" (Motown, blues, Stax records, etc.) from 7:00 to 9:00 pm O'clock where George Banister launched his radio show of exclusively soul music 5 days a week on the "GBS Time" an AM broadcast. All ears were glued to the radio. Out of every home and passing car you heard "GBS Time"! His rating must have sky pocketed but apparently not enough for 4-hour shift or an evening of late night jazz--that we did get from a weak FM signal out of Philly, WDAS.

The North, East and South areas of Trenton all had their levels of danger. My folks tend to mingle with the borderline, less than criminal, types and socially mixed sorts. These were Blacks less fortunate and angry at social conditions they had no economic awareness of—let alone control. Many of them had no say in their destiny, always settling and "makin' do." Periodically, they would lash out in the "hood" with family feuds, fist-fights, razor-cuts, a cuss-by, social disdain and self-hate upon the precious property and people they knew.

Some looked forward to jail-time actually. It was a bed and breakfast resort in the mind of many wayward guys and dolls. Still today, we refer to them as "bad neighborhoods" but in reality, they were oppressed "hoods" who knew not the systemic screws that held them fast to their blights. I'm not blaming any race but Ivan Pavlov, a physiologist and psychologist, scientifically proved almost 200 years ago people behave according their environment. Trenton ghettos got shit and begun to see themselves as the same—shit! Many were led to believe the mystery of the haves and have-nots was their Black fault; not entirely. For example, drugs had not become an epidemic in Trenton in the '60's but Blacks then were blamed for not getting off their asses to find work. Work was there but principally reserved for slacking Chambersburg whites who many chose to be academic bums and school dropouts. What do ya' think the "Fonzie" was pattern after? He was an example of his era and urban time—"Aye!! I'm walkin' here!" With no work anywhere, conveniently drugs fall in the "hood" to be sold anesthetizing feelings of worthlessness and in turn penalizing Blacks for illegally trafficking and selling illegal substances; ultimately painting a picture making Blacks responsible for millions of dollars rags to riches initiation. It being "their fault" was far from the truth.

Many are in jail today because of their lack of knowledge of the law and proper representation, and the political truths that manipulated their existence. How things "fall" into one's neighborhood was not manipulation of their own. They had help.

And then there was Ewing Township, a borough of Trenton. This was a very different class of Negro that we'll spend time on in the next Bouquet Race series that you won't believe. This is where the HBCU grads migrated into their "Jack 'n Jill," Talented Tenth societies, Frats and Sorority clans and debutante balls would hail from.

Chapter 4

"Watchin'"—but not that kind...

Again, Trenton was in rare form on "pay-day," Friday nights— when the "eagle flew higher." Along with our weekend of street observations, came highlight delicacies of deep-fried treats: The soft shell craps, "swimps" (i.e., Shrimp) for my mother, a Porgy fish sandwich dressed with mustard for my dad, a deluxe Philly Double-Cheese-Steak with greasy French Fries and a tall 16oz Royal Crown Cola for me. Like a Blockbuster Movie Marathon, the weekend of "watchin'" da folks and "checkin' out da' scene" was on.

Needless to say, with all those calories, I was a "butterball" of a little fella'. My physical definition was strong but I was robust. My cruel schoolmates would tease my butt that it was ON my back. The days I spent trying to see that in the mirror was contorting. Oh, I was Fat Albert for a number of years. As a matter of fact, I was shaped like that little North Pole "dancing feet" penguin character. LOL. Nevertheless, like him, I had happy little feet in the back seat of Seanna and Steve's big Road Master Buick in need of a dance floor—after my treat. Yes, with all my blubber, I could dance my b'hind off though…and eventually I did. I would take over a party anytime and anywhere. When Noble stepped in the party, the floor started to buckle and the good times were on like popcorn.

So, there I was in the back seat of hog-heaven with my entree of assorted cholesterol samplings of joy and after the food was devoured and the RC Cola gas was dispensed…people watching rapidly became a major bore. The only "watching" that interested me was the next episode of Fred Flintstone or the sweet sound of Mr. Softee, the ice cream custard truck, chiming melodiously from afar. Where? Where?!? Like a hound catching the smell of fallen bacon to the floor, my ears were perched with excitement.

Life was blissfully perfect after a Mr. Softee's custard. Ommm...

Many of my years, looking back, I'd taken life for granted until I realized how much of a building block these learning experiences would pay off later. Just living in Trenton was a character forming skill and a foundation block for observational "watchin'"—but not that kind though, but legally peeking and paying attention to the world and spirits around me. It's the close observation of details that tend to demystify the puzzlement of things. Meaning: I learned that paying close attention was a priceless education. My father would arrest me with, "Close your mouth, open your ears and brain and pay attention, son." "Watching" became a significant power that connected the abstract and the intangibles. By reading my environment, it gave me an uncanny ability to "read people." Much like a psychologist or a medical doctor who reads behavior and pain presentations from a patient, or a judge who reads a defense and prosecution deception, contradiction and misleading hyperbole, one learns to read the body language as well.

Although my folks influenced and instilled this skill in me, I found for myself it requires a code of conduct: what we "read" must come with acceptance and reasonability of what we might glean. What we "read" in others very often can be "cover reading" or speculative assumption without exploration and verification. It can jade the source from which most of us fall victim to. You know: "Judging a book by its cover"? Sometimes what we see is often what we are—a reflection of our own innards, feelings, and inner prejudice, biases, and bigotry. Like racist, they see in an individual, a reflection of something bad, this might actually be something they hate in themselves. False readings has been proven to be dangerous and many people have wrongly gone to jail for it. This is partly why our laws of persecution are based on evidence. Reading the "cover" unfortunately is a lot easier than getting into the "book" which is what many Americans epidemically fall prey to discrimination: people of color, physical stature and even assumed religious differences. Being fair to their "cover," many white people insist to believe Barack Obama is a closet Muslim after FoxNews denigrated his chosen Baptist pastor during his primaries of 2008 with a so-call anti-American 2001 videotape sermon. This "cover" propaganda implied associating views with the pastor supposedly implying Obama a covert enemy of America. A "book" many white people didn't want to read, but opted to fall prey to "cover" judgment. This is classic "cover reading." In the "incriminating" video, as his pastor preaches, he denounces American foreign policy during the George W. Bush administration of lies, manipulation and where its deceptive residuals had "come home to roost." He thought this lead to the bombing of the World Trade Center. The solicitors of this video NEVER journal-honored the source or revile the date of the video sermon, 2001, but exploited it in 2008, conveniently. And, Pastor Jeremiah Wright was labeled "the enemy of the people."

Cover reading, stereotyping and pre-judging are a lot easier. Since it takes so much time to get to know the other guy, or not taking the opportunity to know, we judge the external profiles of the outer shells for pseudo-security convenience. I've found myself altering those very codes, i.e., " the first impression being the lasting impression" which may not always be a healthy code for me or proper assessment for my outlook on others in life. I've shut down many good opportunities by being quickly judgmental.

However, I have made many lifelong friends with a lot of wonderful people who are dear to me; one being the godfather of my son. He's white from Utica, NY, James Bullock. And, the same with my parents who had a smorgasbord of amazing white friends, pals, and well-wishing lovable-buddies, they would limit their affections with handshakes, outburst of good humor and friendly laughter but they risk bringing them home to meet the other white neighbors was chancy and a no, no.

My father worked for a Italian own food goods trucking company, Browns Trucking Company. Get it? Brown's Trucking, it sounds so Italian doesn't it? His boss, Tony, adored Steve and depended on his expertise and attention to detail. But, the only way he could glean information and seek my dad's advice without alarming co-Italian and White workers was to invite my dad over to cut his grass—as a disguised executive-laborer. This way, their social relationship was justified. If Tony's White neighbors felt for a minute he and his non-Italian wife were pressing their "short leash" luck, they would have cause them to feel insecure. Yes, Italians back then were mildly accepted in majority white neighborhoods. But as long as Tony remembered to keep Steve in his place, by cutting his Sunday grass, he was fine with the white neighbors. This was Trenton late to early 1960's.

Later, after the grass was finished, Dad and I would come in to freshen up and sit at her decorated table setting with a mountain of spaghetti and meatballs. Tony, the boss, ate pasta every Sunday with his dear friend Steve, my dad. Surreptitiously by his side, in the privacy of his home, talking business ascertaining my dad's wisdom and knowledge.

My mom and dad's "watching" could detect, characterize individuals unseen and speculate their intent or business at a glance. And most uncanny, my mother's sense of suffering in the poor was especially acute with 95% accuracy. Like a shrewd detective, Seanna could see when a mother or a child was hungry or in need from a distance. She was magically hypersensitive with this super-sense. Speculation aside, "Muhdear" (i.e., mom) would get out of the car to investigate her hunches and verify them with an introduction. Dad too had similar skills but his reaction was slightly different. He'd sympathize with her findings but would not act upon them as gusty as my altruistic mother would. He knew however it was a matter of time he'd be *paying* for some stray puppy nestling in our home while mom coached their "wounds" back to health. He always supported her will to nurture the needy no matter what. Fundamentally, they knew to give abundantly was to receive massively. Since Tony had endowed Steve with handsome weekly pay, they were able to give-back and do their charities of choice. Seanna would randomly approach a needy person out of the crowd, and sure enough, upon introducing herself, she'd discover they were destitute, hungry, abused or both. Actually, I am one of their discovered findings. We will talk more about that later in the series.

I can recall many vagrant souls passing through our four-story home temporarily lodging until their "feet touched the ground again." She would house them, feed them and encourage them by talking straight and honest with them about "life-stuff" they didn't understand or couldn't face, or emotionally couldn't handle. My mother was straighter and harsher than Dr. Phil. Hell, she was Dr. Phil's Grand Mother in this respect. (Seanna Lester below)

10 Seanna, the deaconess, 1980's

She was perceptive yet bold as love. She was a good-hearted "closet thug" of a person and boy was she FO' REAL. She would fight you just as quickly as she would hug you back to health. I'll talk more about her too.

I can remember times feeling disgruntled, jealous and actually heated with resentment toward these vagrant house guests of hers. Because of her benevolence unequal to mine, it seemed to be overwhelming at times; her compassion and concern for them. Although she could see hunger-hurting a mile away, she couldn't understand my silly need for greasy French Fries with a bowl of Kellogg's Frosted Flakes in the middle of the night. What was up wit dat?!? I had needs too mom! I would whine, "They get what they want and I live here!" I would cautiously say that out loud to myself—she also had a swift and non-negotiating backhand and frontal fist pop too. Seanna's general response to my unreasonable mid-night treat request was, "Boy, you betta' get yo' butt in dat bed before I bus' it, heah!" Heck, I needed a hug too.

And ironically, I'd come closer to grips with this outreaching once I

38

weighted the depths of my own orphanage and how that very same home tossed me a life raft to assist a 17-year-old and unfortunate young mother: Blanche Raymond (my biological mother Blanche reunited below with me and my daughter Bianca; look at the likeness.).

11 Noble Lee, Blanche & Bianca Isabel

As high spirited and super sensitive toward mankind as my parents were, they were equally thick-skinned and tough folks that would handle anybody, anything and anywhere—my mom was "Django," the female version of "Django"; without the blood and carnage of course... Well, so I like to believe...

My folks believed that God blesses those who bless others less fortunate. This was the center of their spiritual thinking and philosophical ideology. Helping others was a mantra behavior in our home.

"This ain't something you learn from books, Noble," they both would echo. "Experience is the best teacher on this lesson. You just keep on livin', heah?" Their wisdom showed no bounds, "Everybody gits a chance to be on top and you nevah know when you might be in need. So, when YOU on top you always wanta' do the right thing—and God'll bless ya'." How many times did my mother berate me with those invaluable words of simple wisdom that's paid off so well in my life?

As a teen, I had many friends. My house was the place to get fed- -over-fed actually. There was always something plentiful to eat on Seanna's stove. There were only four of us—with my little-adopted brother Spencer. Cora Lee had moved out and married; ten years my senior; I

was 14 years Spencer's senior.

12 Spencer Lester, 13 years old...?

She'd cook daily like we were an army family. I suppose this was a cultural attribute handed down among Colored folks who believed in fairing for each other during reconstruction, post-slave oppression and segregated hard times. Seanna and Steve remained one of those symbols of Negro Underground Railroad oasis where people like Harriet Tubman on their travels could depend upon I would imagine. Like my parents, many Blacks possess these similar principles and practices in life I would later discover as I matured. You had to look out for each other. It only benefited all to carry somebody else's brother too.

Later, I would graciously join a more progressive conscientiousness of advancing Black snobs in Trenton, the Black middle-class but that too I'll talk more about in the following series.

Chapter 5

If old church folk ran congress for a year

Can you imagine? If we (America) would allow principle based Old School church folk that put humanity, the decency of mankind and the love of God first in their life, ran congress for one year, it would be a better world--I promise you. Would we fuse, fight and carried like-a-fool? Yes! But nevertheless, it would be righteous, decent and in order. For example, Black folks clearly understood the smoke screen of Calvary. Jesus' death was not so much the tragedy. It had to happen so that all would evolve into a blindsided blessing to save mankind. They get that. That being said, I also believe slaves (those old church folk) may have been another flesh-camouflaged smoke screen in chains that God gave America another blindsided gift, another chance, in African people. Look at what happens when you teach Black people positive powers or simply give them a hug of approval, acceptance and extend them appreciation.

I believe with those dormant principals, not quite undisclosed, and un-nationally celebrated, we would find unprecedented measures of real democracy as the Greeks, or perhaps Africans had originally intended. In Black people is innate democracy. What we are experiencing is smoke-screened cultures with angry lyrics, poverty, poison foods consumption, prisons filling, drugs contaminating and gladiator athleticism with too much too soon misdirected wealth that's become the core masking our social

41

gems. I believe if Black church-going organizers could have America for just one year in Congress, this is what we'd see:

1. First, they would shout for joy, halleluiah, that God can make a way out of no way. They'd praise His Holy Name in gratitude that God saw it fit to select them with such a calling. There would be no fights on who would be the speaker of the house but the will of God. Candidates would humble themselves and yield to their favored "Peter" not trash his or her record and call that campaigning. And Judas, by the power of prayer, would remove his self and name himself "strange-fruit."

2. They'd pray sincerely for each session to thank God, not self, or financial contributors, for these many American "blessings." They would put the universal intelligence, God, first. --Even Yoda taught us to respect the universe's "force."--he wasn't black but he was colored.

3. The first order of the day would not be consumed with greed (having more than the next guy) but the security of need: food, shelter, and education for everyone and the knowledge that greed is not a formidable thing especially when you cannot beat God giving.

4. As for science and space travel, that would be no problem. Have you ever seen Michael Jordan, Shawn Kemp, Vince Carter and Dr. Julius Irving dunk?

5. The poor: They would be treated well but also told to "git up off ya' b'hind and git something on your mind. Go do something! Go help others until God helps you. Go to work!" There goes your bipartisan issue—gone.

6. Tithes and offerings (tax) would be equally set for everyone; not the rich paying less and the middle paying more but 10% is 10% and that's that. Africans knew that a plan to be bountiful must include a plan to give back. You reap what you sow--if nothing more than a bigger pot of food on your stove for those that might need.

7. A lobbyist would be too much like a con man to Old School church going folks. They wouldn't stand for that and "God don't favorite it NOR does He like ugly."

8. Just because you have freedom of speech should never mean you have the freedom to talk any way outside of respect. "Yes

ma'am and no ma'am" among Blacks was not spoken in inferiority of master whites but trained respect for eldership. Elders are history tellers (Griots)[2]. Therefore "study your history lessons" or "shut ya' mouth, open ya' ears" and listen to the African-Historian grown-ups—The Griot storyteller was an ancient archival-culture of West -Africa.

9. They would give homage and respect to all leaders with the expectation "too much is given much is required." To share is an act of love.

10. There would be a much bipartisan success because selfish agendas are not the order of the day but "doing the right thing" (pre-Spike Lee) is. That should always be the daily mantra, the call, and the way of life.

11. Again, the nation as one would be taught to respect spiritual leaders and the universe's powers much like the doctrine of every church service across this nation—it's Sunday service everywhere from 11 to 1:00 pm in America and African, time to show homage to the Lord. This Congress would have the people believe worship is for God thereby rendering mankind's peace and continuous joy.

12. Children ain't grown until they are grown-up—got it? Their dress and manners should reflect their maturity.

13. Again, freedom of speech is not the right to say nasty things from your mouth but the freedom to speak your heart under love's grace because the people and our nation's children are listening and learning from our lack of love. They should learn how to get along with each other from tribal leadership and example.

14. Lastly, the tribes WOULD NOT vote for anyone's skin color or his negative campaigning, trashing and spreading hate because that would be endorsing and voting for a damn fool.

The Lester's home today, by my lovely wife and I, still is an Old School watering hole. We try to uphold these above principals and be a social conduit to Black families trying to find their way and a philosophy to live by.

---

[2] a member of a class of traveling poets, musicians, and storytellers who maintain a tradition of oral history in parts of West Africa. --Google

Growing up in Trenton, NJ, I would sometime inadvertently invite bad kids around—I personally didn't like angry, ugly behaving or violent children. Being a thug was never an attraction. They'd turn me off, but some would slip by into my house parties. With my parent's "watchful" sensitivity, observation and character reading abilities, they would easily detect or sense any shady characters quickly—without seeing them.

It is by these memories I discerned with total satisfaction my wonderment of Harriet Tubman and where her character assessment skills hailed from. She must have had to develop such skills to overcome such dire challenges. Transporting bodies to Canada for real freedom must have been beyond the spells of the Hogwart's wand. Ruling out trains, planes, cars, bicycles and interstate passage, she had to attest the first impressions of any potentially threatening person, white or black. Whom could she trust? Whom could she reach out to who were humane, loyal, relied-on and dependable? Ironically, these Northerners would forsake runaways and turn them in back to bounty-hustlers faster than any body-hunter. This is probably how bounty-hunting begin, chasing runaways. Harriet's ability to read people by "watchin'" (sensitive observation) must have been that of a night owl hunting in the night: stealth, quiet, and deadly claws that would take a life instantly. I am sure Harriet was challenged with the same circumstances: white bounty-hunter or snitching house-niggers having to snuff the lights out of disruptive loose-cannon types. What other choice would she have?

Obviously, there were no GPS, few compasses, no accurate maps but just memory of the terrain and the force of the universe's intelligence, God's hand. If you ever wondered why African-Americans are so high spirited, quick to shout for joy, thank the Lord Almighty, called out Hallelujah or praise God's Holy name, wonder no more. We have cause to thank God for his many hugs. 400 years of this American hog-wash has been challenging.

Chapter 6

The Pinkerton Lester's

Steve and Seanna had the uncanny sense of things that "wasn't-quite-right." During my basement parties, unknown visitors of odd sorts would suspiciously unnerve my folks. Once they'd picked-up-on some "bad ass" vibe in the house, they start their parental, inconspicuous prowl; circulating the "beat", if you will. It was like security at Sack 5th Avenue in NYC in the 1980's. Theft detection and racism being what it was then, real white thieves would wait near the front exit for a Black person to exit exiting with them, in full awareness, when the detector alarm sounded the security guard would instinctually suspect and accost the Black person first—I am not joking. My friends and I would often test it. Well, my mom and dad didn't have electric-detectors but they knew people to be inherently thieves or not of good spirit and decency. So, The Pinkerton security patrol would be out in full force discouraging any sleight of hand intention. My mother had been burned before by evil vibes she had ignored. They would not relax until they zeroed in on Mr. or Miss "Bad-ass" and they were out of our house—out of the party—away from their children. They would never embarrass me but I knew something was wrong when the two "sharks" crashed the party and began circling the bloody waters while I tried to get "*my grown and sexy on*"[3] under the basement red light bulb, in da' corner, in the dark. What could I do? It was their house. Announce, "If there are any bad vibes or spirits in the crib, would you please dismiss yourselves, thank you?!" Although they would not announce such a thing their presence among young guppies spoke volumes—and it worked. From that, I learned bad spirits get uncomfortable around kind, positive, loving people and eventually it/they would leave. I've learned it's the fake, phony so-called "loving people" who pretend gets burned.

The power of positive thoughts trumps any negative

---

[3] Hollatainment Records, "Relax," Tenn Stacks, 2008)

contamination 100 fold. The key to defeating negative thinking is NEVER indulging it. And, for your own amusement, observe the negative thinker, or speaker, watch positivity circle back to its positive beginnings. Or, try not to allow one judgmental thought for a ½ hour to see just how positive and strong you are. I've learn that positive thinking is an exercise that strengthens you.

Once "bad-ass" left and my folks felt it, they were cool to retreat back upstairs to their bedroom and finish their evening chill watchin' Perry Mason, Flip Wilson or something. Occasionally, from upstairs, I'd get, "Noble Lee, turn that damn music down some!" But, other than that, the Jimmy-Jam went on like popcorn without a hitch.

I would later learn how elders would anoint their homes with pure olive oil to ward off evil and lingering negative spirits—my wife has done this. They'd dab oil on the door frames, for example. I'm told it's effective—so they believe. Blacks understood this since the beginning, here in the America, there is more to life than just so-called scientific, logical or quantitative evidence that the spirit-world lives.

You have to understand my mom's background as a child-medium. She could actually visualize ghost materializing and dematerializing, coming and going, flying and hiding, good and evil floating through walls, stepping through windows. No, she wasn't a parapsychologist or an apparition paranormal investigator but she was a human EMF meter (i.e., Electric Magnetic Field detector) that could sense paranormal activity and their good and evil intent.

Where she's from, in Georgia, their ghosts were called "Haints," i.e., haunts. She also had the discernment of detecting others who possess such sensitive gifts of good and evil--especially "root people." "Rooters" were people who commonly practice facets of the occult, voodoo (evil), voudou (good), hoodoo, you-do witchcraft or sorcery.

46

13 Recorded ghost images

Chapter 7

Miss Olivia Johnson (Root woman)

On two frightening occasions, my adopting mother (Seanna), a young impressionable woman of the 1940's, was confronted with a root of evil against her.

1.

African American Hoodoo (also known as "conjure", "root working", "root doctoring", or "working the root") is a traditional African American folk spirituality that developed from a number of West African, Native American and later on incorporating European spiritual traditions and beliefs.[4]

Her first root incident was a spell to paralyze her legs while driving, and the other was an attempt on her life--murder. Luckily with both attempts, some root woman was mysteriously and miraculously available to rescue mom and informed her of this occult action and how it was spiritually induced upon Seanna. She advised mom adamantly to "come go with her immediately." Not far, mom, paralyzed, was assisted with the help of some local acquaintance to the root person's home because her legs had actually failed; fallen completely limp. The root-wielding sorcerer was a dark "Asian-for-lookin' woman with slanted eyes," my mother described her in her southern vernacular. The strange woman volunteered her powers to reverse the action of the spell. Mom, although angry and disturbed that someone would actually harm her, stopped her, "No! Don't reverse it." She thought further, "What goes around comes around. 'Vengeance is mine saith the Lord.'"[5] She remembered and continued, "Can you tell me who did this?"

---

[4] Wikipedia, Hoodoo folk magic, 2016
[5] Roman 12:19

The root woman asks, "What's your name?"

My mother replied, "Seanna...Seanna Sally Lester"

The root woman requested, "Place a penny on this playing card and call the name of Jesus." So, mom did so and the root woman uttered some inaudible prayer-like words, perhaps a speaking in tongues...?

She then asks mom, "Turn the card over there you will see the face of the speller—the conjurer."

Mom did as the root woman had instructed and to her complete shock, low and behold, a picture of a woman appeared... It was a dimensional hologram-like image—she described—of a woman from the neighborhood to whom she admired as a sweet lady and a friendly social acquaintance.

The root woman restated, "Are you sure you don't want revenge?"

Mom replied, "No. I know this woman. That's Miss Johnson... Olivia Johnson... She's my friend... Why would she do something like this to me? You sure?"

The root woman prophetically offered, "She's hurting with jealousy, baby. You have too much... more than she. She cannot stand it."

Given the era and time, this doesn't strike me odd because during the early 20th-century destitution was a designed way of life. It was orchestrated for the Negroes to accept and live within a land of hypocritical freedom with convenient economic glass ceilings—the buck and the Negro stopped there. Fortune was not afforded to Negroes by design. And, poor whites were encouraged NOT to tolerate Blacks of seemingly higher station—these were ugly times for white people. I cannot for the life of me wrap my head around such angry-racial-supremacy. Crack-heads get better treatment today than turn of the 20th Century Negroes did.

As a result, Blacks begun to systemically envied each other snitching and crab-clinging (obstruction). This was commonplace among even close-knit Black communities—families even. It was an innate negative lifestyle among the Coloreds. These House-Negro informants would bring information to Whites who abhorred uppity stations of Coloreds. And, "Crackers" types, as they were called and embraced, were poor, illiterate and uneducated led to believe they were better than Negroes nonetheless, no matter their profession. Equally, many Whites in the south were oppressed and transient accounting for many cowboy stagecoach robberies, rowdies and hoodlums. Many, Quakers mainly, would resist hatred toward Blacks of higher station. Some respected Negro-professions or business enterprising. But, for many, these higher stations would rub most "Crackers or "Redneck"[6] wrong. Whites would call these white lesser stations, "trash" and they express their angst toward Negroes with rage, jealousy and violent anger. A professional Black-man somehow made them suffer inferiorities. These very same whites would be taken advantage of by superiors. They were illegally and shrewdly coerced into ill-fated racist activities that benefited upper bigot driven political schemes: burning churches, stealing livestock, arrest Blacks for J-walking, looking at white women and robbing farm land crop.

The "Grapes of Wrath" (a film about American depression) depicted the white and poor in America. Many poor Whites honored their lot-in-life, their station, during those years. Many actually embrace their status--really. They coexisted with the Coloreds. "We're just regular God-fearin' po' folks" was a mantra among MANY White people before the 1990's and again they were proud to give their life at war; proud to labor and work hard in coal mines and for minimum wages; proud to make-do with what they had; a possum in every pot was ideal living. But, to get by with their lack, and political powers that be, they had to politically and socially express some hate toward the Negro. Coexistence was all good until the evils of the Klan, wayward backwoods preachers and politicians

---

[6] Whites were called Rednecks because they too had to work next to Slaves in the fields and burning sun.

swayed them otherwise.

And, often Negroes would sell each other out; hurt and hinder each other as a lifestyle. There is a long historical culture of house-niggers ratting other out for far less than 30 pieces of silver--pewter even. These were awful times when people actually feared for their lives if a fellow Negro was progressive or made educational headway or enterprising leaps. Real trust won't permeate among Negroes until the 1960's and civil rights movements. It took a while before Blacks appreciated leaders like Dr. Martin Luther King, Jr. In my own household, many feared rousing racists Whites. They thought this protesting activity would make life harder for the state of peace Coloreds had thus far ascertained. Many were just beginning to learn to accept and socially tolerated their segregated lot in life.

There is quite a barometric change in the atmosphere among white people when they collectively grow angry. You can actually feel it in the air, e.g., the bombing of Pearl Harbor, the assassination of Kennedy, the verdict of OJ Simpson and the election of Obama, etc. You could feel the presence of their dread. What was a Negro to do when such a force fell upon them?

It was a time that bored a debilitating distrust among Blacks that dug deep in their hearts. To this day, some still lament that "a 'n-word' ain't sh**!" "A n-word just won't do right for nothing." Much of this stems from runaway snitching. Frightened slaves were informants to ease the backlash of escapees and the accused collusion, "running to tell dat to massa" or "run and tell that!"are common colloquial expressions. I remember hearing these awful words as a child, and adulthood. It was said matter of factly to each other with murmuring agreement.

I upset and embarrassed my father while among his buddies and tribal council with a deflating question and challenge. Now, even though my father detests the "n-word," he agreed strongly that Blacks could be non-compliant, non-productive and worthless. So, my embarrassment came with a confrontation in front of his agreeing friends. I shared with them an arrogantly presented question. "If an n-word ain't sh**, does that mean we all here ain't sh**?" After all, they endearingly referred to each other as n-word comrades. So in this context, where's the harm? Well, there was a hushed pregnant-pause that fell over them like a dark cloud from the Barad-dur castle from the Hobbit movie. Although my father, a naturally quiet spirit, began to boiled over like a tempted fire-breathing dragon. He grew furious that I'd challenged his extending hard-fast paradigm of cultural thinking toward Black people on the carpet. How dare I, in front of his boys, confront him with the truth of his self-applied stigma and esteem lowering affirmations...? He didn't appreciate the disrespect but he was stumped by the truth of his unconscious worth-cancer that wormed ramped among his peers.

I can only imagine they all labeled me a little shit thereafter. But, back to the root-woman, she continued, "This woman will come to you again and she will come to borrow a cup of sugar." She strangely predicted, "She'll probably be surprised to see that you're not dead, hurt or at least very ill but say nothing just give her the sugar. She'll return again to pay you back the money she owes you also."

"What?!?" my mother thought. This knowledge completely floored her with panic and fear. What, with an actual neighbor planning her demise, and worse, a stranger totally predicting its outcome. This was too much.

My mother had actually forgotten the $10 loan. She was in shock at the Root-woman's level of mysticism and the prophetic knowledge gotten out of the air. "How could the Asian for-lookin'-woman just know these things," she freaked?

The root woman continued, "But, don't touch it. She will lace it with a harmful dust. So, give the money away, to anyone, it won't hurt them. And, say nothing to this woman."

My mother felt deeply the warning and danger the root woman was conveying. Sure enough, days later Miss Johnson actually knocked on the front door after my mom had begun relaxing to the whole ordeal of confronting her or this prediction playing in real-time, doubting it would even happen, wondering if the Asian-Gypsy woman had hustled her, or set her up for future exploits. But, when mom opened the door, to her chagrin, there she stood. A nervous shock riddled through my mother's body. Miss Olivia also visibly flinched with surprise and an air of disappointment. She pretentiously went into a festival of grins. And just as predicted, she pretended to utter her need to borrow a cup of sugar nervously...! Wow!! This fortuitously creep my mom out. It took every nerve in her body to stealth the panic she felt in her gut. Could Miss Johnson perhaps see or sense her fear like a Jeeper Creeper? Hear her heart pounding like a xenomorph? Seanna had to think quickly. Here stood her murderer in color.

"Oh Miss Olivia! Chiild, I am plum out. I got to get some mo' when Steve come home. I used the last for his coffee this morning. I am so sorry."

The next day, on cue, she returned with the money she had borrowed as prophesied. This time she knocked on the screen door a second time.

"Hello, hello. Seanna?"

My mother is very afraid now and very nervous for her life replied, "Yes?"

"It's Olivia, baby. Can I come in?"

"Ah, I, ah, just waxed my flo'. I, I cain't come to the front right now. What you want, mam?"

"Oh, I'm so sorry. I have ya' money I got from ya' befo'."

"Oh! ...Thank you. ...Just put it on the dressah (dresser) by the do' (door), okay?"

"...I can come around the back and put it in ya' hand."

Whoa!! My mother's body shivered fighting back the dreaded panic and fear she felt, "Ahm, I just waxed the back linoleum flo' too. Like a silly fool, I done waxed myself into a corner. (LOL) I am so, so sorry."

"...That's okay, I've done the same thing; you do keep it so nice."

"Thank you. It'll be alright there on the dressah and I'll git it soon as the flo' dry. Thank you, mam, heah?"

"...Oh no, thank you. Alright, den. Here it is yonder. Thank ya', baby. Bye."

"Okay."

All the while my mother was standing nearby clutching a butcher's knife terrified and ready to strike if Olivia had crossed that threshold defiantly. My mother later burned the $10 and the dolly cover from the dresser top as well. She sanitized the dresser top with "hot-scolding" water and lye soap. She treated those ten dollars like the department of CDC; like anthrax from a virus Petri-dish. Miss Olivia never crossed paths with my mother again. She just disappeared into her home like a reclusive hermit crab she'd proven to be.

Miss Johnson extreme feelings of jealousy weren't unwarranted. My parents as young lovers were very fortunate—unprecedentedly so. They had ascertained great wealth uncommon to Negroes during these times in the south. My father Steve until he died had many white bosses that always adored his friendliness, loyalty and hard work saw that Steve was well provided for.

By the way, there are some clear distinctions among Black folks. If you were "**colored**," this denoted you were a socialized laborer. You were deemed common, probably mildly-illiterate and church-going who'd ritualistically fumbled their way through the bible's reverence and antiquated King James language.

If you were "**Negro**," this generally denoted you were perhaps educated, professional, progressive, politically conscious and generally of lighter-skin and complexion.

Again, this was a compliant unspoken culture, enforced and maintenance by both whites and blacks mutually. "**House-niggers**" served as a two edged blade. Although, serving as intel for the outside shack-dwelling niggahs and then they were informants charged to be nosey and snitch on Blacks and their religious/political underpinnings reporting to the "white-authorities." They were cultural Judas who were never wholeheartedly welcomed. And, they often lost their lives being too familiar and snooping too much in white affairs. Vicariously fooling themselves, they were somehow included among their privileged masters. They sadly found themselves hanging from the end of a noose, if they knew too much: white's opiod and alcohol use, infidelity, deviant sexual behavior, bastard off-spring children by slaves and hidden crimes.

In time, powerful efforts were socially laid, laws later put into place to ensure that Negroes were not obstructed in social and political advancements. MLK, Jr. harassed President Lyndon Baines Johnson for many years to get him to executively move on civil rights issues, but even that was a slothful tide sanctioned and mandated by law. Legislating the hearts and minds of stubbornly bias white men and women was another heavy load entirely.

My birth place, Valdosta, Georgia, was small and it had very little, if any industry, to offer the "Negro" families then. My folks in spite of many odds, spiritual, racial or otherwise did very well in spite of economic depression. But still there were Othello targets for the many "Iago's" in this Shakespearean-like arena. Things were tough there for the mid-20th century Negroes where even a Desdemona might turn you in for 30 pieces of silver.

Chapter 8

Le Noir Classicism

Your limited business prospects back then were farming, smoked or BBQ swine sales. They collect and sold pecans, raised chickens and hens in the south. Many Black men were trained construction workers thanks to the HBCU vocational institutions like roofing, cement laborers, asphalt spreading, masonry block, brick, and stone. Hair cutting and hair styling (Hot comb hair pressers) was a sure way for women to survive. White women weren't coming to Colored or Negro hair stylist then nor did Black women allow or wanted to use White hair stylist—they were completely different worlds.

Sewing alterations and dressmaking were prosperous for Black women. They were amazingly prolific—this was a necessary home-economic skill taught in the most homes. Blacks could not afford or were allowed to peruse boutiques and browse among high-fashion quality stores. So, the knack for sewing by window-shopping was a necessary sight skill to self-teach. Before the outsourcing of Asian sweatshops and cheap labor, Colored women manufactured textile houses and learned the craft of sewing. They would create a lot of worldly fashions in the 1940's and '50's for men and women that would get outright stolen. Whites and immigrants would steal Black designs without any fear of infringement and sadly many Blacks felt honored that something creative of theirs made the highlight cut of fashion even though their names weren't credited to it.

Mid-wives and some internal medicine-men (physicians) were the community's civil brightest. There could only be a few dispensed about the surrounding counties. Colored doctors and their wives was the elitist. These physicians had to be certified by state and county. This came with prestigious honors and community respect. To ascertain such a calling, this required passing board tests. This made Negroes exceptional and proud—often called and labeled by whites: "a credit to their race."

Outlets of physical labor were plentiful: shipping, hauling, field picking, assembly lines, etc both south and the north. There was much labor to go around but unfortunately a coin-toss fell in favor of poor Whites in those days—they were the first to be hired. Blacks were the first to be fired. Blacks did not fight this favoritism for survival sake. White priority and first chosen practices was a reality—even if he was [7]"John Henry" himself, white tunnel diggers came first. There was a cultural guarantee for any poor White looking for work, he would be considered first—and that was okay with everyone. This drew less tumultuous attention to vulnerable Coloreds. Today it is not so much glass-ceiling preferential issues of labor but similar prejudice transmuting to wealth privileges— cash flow and banker's backing—which also went first to Whites and Euro-American immigrants.

Ironically, Coloreds preferred this status simply because of White men, financially or emotionally deprived, was an imminent threat to Blacks. Blacks getting privileged opportunities soon attracted the Klan. A deprived White man was the husband that kicked the cat, beat the wife and screamed at the children and Black families represented all 3. Any threat to whites' preferential treatment resulted in cop-shootings, rape, drunken attacks, property vandalism, arson and random explosions, etc.

Preaching or pasturing, this was the hierarchy of respect among Negro and Colored communities back then. They were often regulated and limited in scope by a few churches prior to the 1970's in the south. There were few preachers certified to go around—actually whites would appoint their ministry not the congregation. Either pastors were grandfathered-in or politically ordained by white sanction and religious registration, or they actually assisted the Negro clergies to their parish. In other words, a white male field hand was paid to monitor all church serves. One could preach but he was given a territory of a wide but limited radius. One preacher would lend himself out to several county churches per Sunday, per month covering a radius of several miles. Although you

---

[7] https://en.wikipedia.org/wiki/John_Henry_(folklore)

had thousands of churchgoers with many who were more than capable of pasturing, Whites weren't keen on too many spiritual leaders. Heretofore, leadership threatened the possibility of conscious-rearing, civil protest, rallying, revolution, financial strength, social voting ideas or political strength and underground railroads.

Here lately, the opposite ministerial effects have taken hold with too many Baptist churches diminishing Black numbers to be less assembled. They are now becoming religiously divided and far less politically empowering because of lacking numbers of legitimate members to go around and the PEOPLE getting too many different directives. This is strategically due to quasi-college certificate pastors whom ironically are now getting by with easy Divinity Degrees or online clergy-training. They are "unaccredited degrees" from so-called accredited maw and paw White chaired religious training institutes who prey and capitalize on the confidence of young pastors who are anxious to do God's will. Currently, 2016, there were 2500 Baptist churches in Jacksonville Florida alone to date. 70% of them are Black churches.

Whites did not want, or allow, Blacks to have too much political power and influence over parishioners. Again, a preacher in one place too long was a threat to white control and maintenance over Blacks. They kept them moving even though their Emancipation and 13th amendment rollouts had legally bound their feet to granting Blacks their rightful freedom. These were the devious ways they continued to obstruct Blacks.

Mom and Dad Lester did what they had to do to "make-do" (survive) and live. My folk's unprecedented fortune drew inevitable fits of resentment from other Blacks. Can you imagine being hated because you had a little more money or you made a living or purchased a contemporary vehicle, i.e., a Cadillac? My parents were blessed-sheep with pork chops necklaces among bankrupt wolves --trying to survive social contempt.

Education was at a premium accomplishment among some

culturally driven Black communities. High school graduates actually taught high school back then. My biological great-grandmother Leila Mae Barfield (the woman on the opening page of this book with my grandfather Orson Barfield) was an away teacher. Much like the pastors, she was sent away for the week to other counties to teach, and come the weekend, she'd maid white homes at night or the weekend leaving her own daughter Blanche (bio-parent) home to fend for herself. It was unthinkable to have a bachelors or master's degree to teach remedial level corrective education in Black communities of the 1930's thru the '60's—no way, whites wouldn't allow it. This was all by intended socio-political design.

So it did not help for my adopted mother's (Seanna) step-brother, Reverend Robert B. Logan to be an unfinished 2nd year college student and the darling womanizer of Jacksonville, Pensacola, St. Mary and Valdosta's finest either; as he strutted his stuff in he's pristine starched U.S. Army uniform and spit-shined shoes proudly through white

downtown.

14 Daisy & Will Foster, bottom right. Robert Logan, top right with black vest and tie (Afro) and wife Gladys. Allen Henderson, bottom center with black tie white shirt and wife Gladys.

He was saluted by a few for his service but strutting for some, black and white, was brazen, braggadocios and flat-out uppity. But, my family didn't give a shit about anyone's contempt. In fact, that caused them to pour it on.

The "PH's" were people who psychologically thwarted or obstructed the advancement of other Black progress. *Player-Haters* abhorred the Foster/Logan family not only roadblock and tried to hold them back, for reasons and habits unknown to them, but just for the hell of keeping them unhappy. Blacks never quite grasp why they'd assist the oppressors. Perhaps it was that rock and hard place they found themselves in wanting desperately to be apart and included by white America that never came. Quentin Tarantino's creation of Negro concierge, "Stephen Candy," in the movie "Django," who pandered, snitched, covertly informed, bullied as the big-house's overseer or HNIC. A head-nigger-in-charge was a man or woman the Black community feared and despised. The HNIC would arrogantly sought after the approval of white people ONLY. His job was not to care about the welfare of other slaves. I can only say that American history has lied drastically to the Negroes, Coloreds and Blacks.

My uncles Allen Henderson and Rev. Logan were esteemed building contractors of homes and industry. And, they were very active and quite successful in the <u>white</u> communities. To some Blacks, this was an anomaly, perhaps a freak of nature that they were stepping in this kind of "high cotton." Some "PH's" loathed the idea. They despised the thought of their "social-competitor" getting ahead of them in this futile fight for white acceptance and approval. Believe it or not Ripley, Negroes would fight over who was going to be titled "the first."

To further add to their inane jealousies, my adopted grandmother (Momma Daisy Foster, sister's child of Seanna's mother became Seanna's adopted guardian after her mother's death.) owned the one and only 50-mile radius soul food eatery in the Black section of town. To boot, she also possessed long, straight, "jet black" Indian, Seminole, hair that fell long to her waist. This was a time when Blacks violently rejected nappy hair quality. They wanted no parts of looking African. In fact, they detested it. Again, trying to assimilate and fantasized the likeness of European straight hair. The community women hated Momma Daisy's Indian-born attributes. It was a DNA miscegenation Daisy wasn't entirely aware of but that didn't matter. She was closer to looking like a white woman than her tribe did. Daisy's Indian locks were the closest hair quality to that of a white woman: thick, rich and refined. This envy would curdle the blood of her Black competitors during those times. It's no doubt Seanna's "hit-woman," Olivia Johnson, thought someone should pay for all this "out of place" fortune that Olivia could never have.

These were predictable social after effects common with any racial or ethnic group. Oppressing people is dangerous for everyone. There are no win-win outcome with self loathing because one's color or hair quality is irrelevant. To hate self is debilitating and environmentally destructive for all. It's a brush fire blown randomly by crossing winds. Mixing mice with limited cheese in their red-lined urban maze are nothing less than "deprived rodents" who will begin to eliminate each other for survival sake. Unconsciously and without full knowledge of their moral actions, they will annihilate each other.[8]

When it comes to these psychological profiles, I find unprecedented lack of empathy for the Africans as well as Native-Americans. Their maladjusted outcries, social ills of lacking coalition and criminal options are too many.

Any student of sociology can qualify without a doubt how such pressures on the oppressed could warrant stereotypical outcomes and ill-fated manifestations on Black society. Just as 241 years (1776 thru 2017) of Founding Father's paradise has given whites a sense of invincibility, once they found the confidence to defeat mother England, has equally thwarted those under the same duress. Watching the British red coattails

---

[8] Ivan Petrovich Pavlov verified this theory in the 1800's.

tucked between their legs running scared, did something for American settler's ego. Well, 400 years of slavery has given Blacks a sense of mental dead-end apathy with opposite effect on their egos. Blacks know these oppressive social effects are without ethnic and race base; any race or nationality can suffer such depletion and depression. However, those excuses aren't afforded to Blacks. We can't claim "Holocaust" or Armageddon or Syrian refuge. But ironically, here lies a testament of truth of Black's indefeasible African strength. The African yet manages and continues to rise with his mind "regulated," his "soul-saved" and "sanctified in the blood." These affirmations that have sustain the halls of spiritual believers, proves it is God's will that they must survive.

The north side of Jacksonville, Florida, was the land of the Logan family. Yes admittedly, they had a tendency to **flaunt** their wares, strut-their-stuff and peacock about. Now, this didn't help cross-the–board racist backlash. But, let's face it, my families were arrogant "Field-Negroes" made good. They weren't quite as bad as Samuel L. Jackson's "Stephen Candy" de Negro but they were more like the "Unchained" pit bulls. And boy, did they know it. They were overly sure of themselves. Hubris isn't a nice enough term to describe them here.

We'll talk more about that later in the coming series. But, back to Miss Olivia...

Chapter 9

Back to Olivia

Seanna did finally confront the caster of her evil spells and she did something I will always hold in great respect and honor. She exercised something far from the reach and growth of most humans. She forgave this woman for her nefarious behavior. I'm not certain if I could have filtered such a noble disclosure of righteousness after all her devious attempts. For some, forgiveness is hard. I work on it daily. It's difficult but it's had a serious effect on me. It often feels like the "other guy" is getting away with something when I try to pretend to forgive. By me forgiving, I feel they're getting off scot-free without any justice or punishment. I'm still trying to forgive my best-man who showed up drunk with his boom-box and begun club-serenading a woman while my wife and I stood yet in the alter with the officiant waited to conclude. LOL. Every time I see this dude I have to remind myself, "He's just an idiot and he doesn't know any better."

I wrestle with their only having to say, "I'm sorry." "Pardon me." "I don't know what I was thinking." "The devil made me do it. "It was a moment of weakness or passion." It is by this I have so much respect for Black people in this country forgiving the things that white-terrorist have done, and still do. We Americans can sing out, "The British are coming," but dare not lament, "The Klan won't leave." The Klan actually express their disdain if Blacks protest or complain about having to "take a knee" to signify that Black lives do matter. They kill Black men and boys during our millennium, while carrying a badge. This is flat wrong. Yes, I salute Black people for their uncanny gifts for forgiveness.

I've learned from my mom that forgiveness is an exercise of closure that is rendered unto the "forgiver," not the forgiven. It's for me that I forgive that I might release the burning coals in my heart that only I carry around night and day: on my face, in my spirit, in my attitude that causes me negative stress contaminating others; loving innocent people a lot less than loving them more. It causes unhealthy high blood pressure, bad teeth, and other physical dangers and deteriorations. The relief of cancerous disdain becomes mine when I forgive. It's one of the few times we are actually God-like—when we forgive.

Mom reports that Miss Johnson fell to her knees in shame that day begging for forgiveness quite pitifully; confessing her jealousies had fallen to hate because of her own misfortune of being child barren and husbandless. Mom resisted painstakingly. She was overwhelmed with empathy but the need to "co-cop" or "slap da' piss outta her" also entered her mind strongly as the woman repented tearfully. It was probably there, right then, forgiveness allowed mom to embrace her in a hug. This one gesture refueled Miss Johnson with the affection she desperately and perhaps unconsciously longed for. In an instant, my mother hugged away impending spirits of demons rotting at this woman's very core with purges of joy through forgiveness.

Did the cause of spells and root practices ever really ended for my young parents? Yes, but it made them leery, more hyper-aware and watchful of the "real world" of dangers around them. They woke up to what was happening in the hearts and souls of Black people in the scary south and their children. Whether it was self-hate conjuring or systemic racism, the atmosphere was never good for anyone. There wasn't much my folks could do but try the "liberated north."

"They had learned to watch as well as pray." Prayer began an engraved practice with them growing up. "Keep your eyes open" became a metaphor for learning to anticipate, perceive and accept life's peculiar ways--but what of the unforeseen? The Colored root-worker or white Klansman? "Six in one hand, ½ dozen in the other." Are some racist *ways* of behavior modifying? ...They're getting better with slothful progress, yes. Will its aftereffect of hardship end with time? Perhaps. Will young whites and blacks make a new frontier for their children be the antidote?—I don't know but I pray like hell so. Perhaps the tool of prayer and paying close attention to details, vibes and spirit undercurrents will be the meditation of the day that cures our fragile to broken hearts. Perhaps, pettiness like jealousies and prejudice offers only kinetic and potential devastation that we might one day be free of.

The world tells all when and if we but shut-up and listen with bated breath. Mother-nature speaks volumes. She is telling us just what to do. So, for the good of the American family's spiritual health, we accept that gaining her wisdom and understanding that life will have its challenges no matter what or where we are. Fears are never the catalogue that forges us ahead to civil Minerva.

With that, the Lester's migrated north to more denser populated cities with greater numbers where small-town grudges did not prevail so readily—so they thought. Our parents took me and their biological child (Cora Lee) to higher and safer ground--so they desired to believe. Their first stop was Atlantic City, NJ. There they discovered struggling European immigrants socially suffering much like southern Blacks, if not worst— Hell's Kitchen[9] similarities, Little Italies and China Towns, etc. They too were discriminated, red-lined and less tolerated by white-mainstream. I can remember as a child when mainstream Americans thought it strange to eat bagels, Lox, pastrami, Tahini sauce, lamb, using olive oil, canned sardines and dining with corn-beef & cabbage or kielbasa-sausage. Americans eat meat and potatoes and maybe some green peas.

However, French cuisine, vacationing in Paris and foreign fashion was the rage, highly advocated and accepted. I remember when learning French was a requirement in school among the elite White children; Colored children didn't test substantially well enough to qualify for such academic reaching, or other European languages for that matter— certainly not German. And, Kiswahili, a universal African language, that was completely out of the purview of academic discussion—most HBCU's today aren't discussing African language curriculums.

I'll never forget my excited Nigerian professor colleague at Edward Waters College sharing with me his newly published book as he entered my office elated with a hop in his step, "400 dialects and languages of Africa" he'd published. My jaw dropped when he shared so casually the average African speaks at least 10 foreign European languages and most of the African dialects were described in his book.

Northern Americans like Southerners back then would educationally deprive Coloreds and Negroes. It was clear Whites intrinsically believed Blacks were inferior to them. It was often infuriating to

---

[9] Decadent European slums of mostly NYC but other cities. Dictionary.com 2016

observe that Michelle and Barack both were double Ivy League graduates never acknowledged and ignored by white racist. What's ignorant is to be driven by racism, bigotry, and bias and not to realize the universe is "no respecter of person." God does not favor race. Apparently God choose everyone, not just Israel. Everything is perishable under the sun and no one is better than the other. It's a fact. There was one Larry Bird and many Harlem Globe Trotters, this is not to conclude that white-men can't jump. It is evil's misleading trap to get us to think otherwise.

For Blacks, there were times when they couldn't tell the social differences between the Mississippi south or the NJ north. Even the immigrates would assimilate with such "white behavior" conforming fraternally with racial bias—just for a promissory piece of the American pie—Jews would straighten their noses, dyed their hair blond and "perming" their hair straight. Lebonese, Italians, Greek, eastern-Indian immigrants begun seeing themselves as white people.

Racism is a spiritual illness that gets worse. It socially spreads contaminating others with like mindless evils. Granted our American societies are slowly learning how to bully less, maybe gun sales will soon follow, socially accepting others more and becoming less afraid of so-called "differences" in races and less guilty for social crimes against others, will bring on a better difference in us all. But, still many are vastly affected by associated ignorance. Racism is ignorant. There was/is no amount of alcohol, painkillers, gambling, excessive spending or crystal meth to ease these guilt-driven pains that whites suffer as a result of social hate. These mindsets of guilt can and are cancerously eating at our society's core. Until reconciliation, confession and repentance takes a fundamental hold on this paradigm of negative thinking, on some level, be it socialism, liberalism, welfare or altruism, we might not ever redeem our peace, love and find time to get or give a hug.

Hollywood is getting better but they were once out of hand: Elizabeth Taylor as "Cleopatra," Yvonne De Carlo as "Zipporah," "Anne Baxter as "Nefertari," Lawrence Olivier as "Othello," Joseph Fiennes pending to play Michael Jackson in a so-called British film dated for a 2016 opening—BBC? Sounds like a more racist cover-up. Sidney Poitier, a native Bahamian, of Coco Island, was not the only iconic Negro actor[10] of his time in his lot. In fact, thespian Negroes of Harlem, Newark, DC, Baltimore, Memphis, New Orleans, Kansas City, Atlanta, Jacksonville LaVilla, Savannah, Philly and L.A. all contribute to training this island farmer-boy both his deep Caribbean dialect, speech and acting crafts.

Hollywood feared, much like today's Oscar prejudice, that racist Whites would not respond positive with good ticket sales with too many Blacks faces onboard.

Chapter 10

Reprise: "Watchin'"

In any event, Cora Lee and I as children would continue our studies in "watching" and "reading" people, groups, and crowds for survival sake. My sister became a champion reader direct from our mother's DNA. Cora could read a thug, a liar and crazy people a mile away. In fact, because of her acute skills, she became one of Trenton State Psychiatric Hospital's top psychiatric assistance for the paranoid/schizophrenic and criminally insane in the state of NJ for 27 years where her son is currently employed, in the very same position. Myself, well, became a playwright, actor, and director a observer of motive and character for the stage and screen.

---

[10] See historical Black actor list of the 1950 & the '60's:
http://www.blackpast.org/tree/Actors/Actors

15 Noble (10) & Cora far left Sonny, Mom & Dad right

16 Cora & I older back at the Atlantic Ocean beach 1980.

This is my overture for the Bouquet Race series. It's my presentation for the well being of non-indigenous Africans who struggle for their essence among the tapestry of American life. It is my opening for a forthcoming tsunami of hopefully sweet verbiage of wisdom on loving all Americans but mostly healing Blacks, Africans, Brothers, and sisters with love; not disdain, lack-of-privilege, segregation or police bullets but with real affection.

All ills aside, we/they, Black people just need a hug like any recovering ancient genocidal victim. This book(s) is not exclusively about "watching" and "reading" the masses—but it is exclusively about healing one part of the American family, the African-Americans part. It's my guess until they all feel included; upon their long servitude existence. It won't get "better."

This series of books are specifically about the evolution of their experiences, their un-researched African origins, street smarts, intuition all empirically woven together to say we matter also. Of course, all lives matter but only Blacks are being beat-down, gunned down more and are hugged less. It's clear their angry... just listen to the young and their rap music—they're pissed off frankly. Do they sound like Motown and their once festive pastoral lyrics of love? Hell, no! Have you heard about Blacks and their horrendously lethal levels of blood pressure suffering? Does that sound like people whom intrinsically feel they are included, Kum-ba-yah?

They are not being invited fellowship or tenured at the Ivy-tables, to the banker's-table, political power-tables, sport owners-table, manufactory or industry-tables or dinner table to eat welcomingly. Politically, pitifully, tokens yes. Langston Hughes would often poetically lament how he was asked to "Eat in the kitchen when company comes."

Surely, every man must pull his own shoe straps up to earn an included place at the American halls, monuments and family tables—I couldn't agree more. But, in this case, they could use a real less than metaphoric embrace for coming this far co-existing with racist white people in this marathon of a metropolis races. In the one country that fights foreign terrorism tooth and nail except inside its own Klu Klux Klan backyard.

African-Americans don't see white stage-plays, white movies, white-TV, European-restaurants, white-retail, business or Disneyland as white amusements only. They see these wonders of America as their own, their home and all the rightful freedoms thereof.

What do I hope to accomplish in the forthcoming series? I will observe theories that might apply to the improvement of developing American as a whole with Blacks "included." We will explore self-love, sustained joy and harmonic tactics in our ever-battling kick-ass grope for national happiness.

Comparatively, this overture is light stuff during my childhood. It was a different time that has personally taught me to be about self-esteem and health for our "bouquet of brown skin" continuum. Of course, one does learn from just "watching," but praying and paying attention to life and all its perilous dangers but more importantly praising the good that lives in us all.

Luke 21:36

"Watch, therefore, and pray always that you may be counted worthy to escape all these things that will come to pass, and to stand before the Son of Man."

Song of Solomon 8:6

Set me as a seal upon your heart, as a seal upon your arm, for love is strong as death, jealousy is fierce as the grave. Its flashes are flashes of fire, the very flame of the LORD.

The End

To continue this series purchase

Charter I and the following series: II thru IX

Of

The Bouquet Race

Brown People Adored (History and "OURSTORY," told)

On Amazon.com/KindleBooks

http://www.amazon.com/Bouquet-Race2-People-Adored-ebook/dp/B00BRHZ8RA/ref=pd_ybh_3

17 Biological families: Lizzie & Solomon reunion 2011

To my dear Lizzie and Solomon derived family tree ancestry.

And I dedicate this to my loving wife Lena Annette & our wonderful children:

Tara, Nikki, Jovita, Nabila Lee, Ivan Ray, Noble Lee, II (Tenn Stacks) and Bianca Isabel Lester that one day they will read these words and know some truth of our love for their future with all Americans.

To my beloved big sister who actually helps me to survive most of it all with belief in me, lending her car, a sofa I was always welcomed to and the way she'd introduce me proudly to everyone, "This is my Bruhda'," and her kind smile.

NOTES:

The Bouquet Race: My Overture